Animals at the...
Pet Shop

Siân Smith

Raintree

Raintree is an imprint of Capstone Global Library Limited, a company incorporated in England and Wales having its registered office at 7 Pilgrim Street, London, EC4V 6LB – Registered company number: 6695582

www.raintreepublishers.co.uk
myorders@raintreepublishers.co.uk

Text © Capstone Global Library Limited 2015
First published in hardback in 2014
The moral rights of the proprietor have been asserted.

Edited by Siân Smith, John-Paul Wilkins and Helen Cox Cannons
Designed by Cynthia Akiyoshi
Picture research by Mica Brancic and Tracy Cummins
Production by Victoria Fitzgerald
Originated by Capstone Global Library
Printed and bound in China

ISBN 978 1 406 28053 1
18 17 16 15 14
10 9 8 7 6 5 4 3 2 1

British Library Cataloguing in Publication Data
A full catalogue record for this book is available from the British Library.

Acknowledgements

We would like to thank the following for permission to reproduce photographs: Shutterstock pp. 1 (© Igor Kovalchuk), 2 (© Andrew Burgess), 3 left (© Jagodka), 3 middle (© Smit), 3 right (© kontur-vid), 4 (© Africa Studio), 5 (© Hannamariah), 6, 21 (© AlexKalashnikov), 7 (© DmZ), 8 (© rkucharek), 9 (© My Good Images), 10 (© Sarycheva Olesia), 11 (© vovan), 12, 22b (© Brian Lasenby), 13 (© Kamonrat), 14 (© Oleksandr Briagin), 15 (© Anna Kucherova), 16 (© xpixel), 17 (© Jill Lang), 18 (© Shcherbakov Ilya), 19, 22a (© irin-k), 20 top left (© Rich Carey), 20 top right, 20 bottom right (© Eric Isselee), 20 bottom left (© Feng Yu).

Front cover photograph of a hamster reproduced with kind permission of Shutterstock (© Alex Kalashnikov).

Every effort has been made to contact copyright holders of material reproduced in this book. Any omissions will be rectified in subsequent printings if notice is given to the publisher.

Contents

Pet shop animals

Will you get a cat?

Will you get a dog?

Will you get a hamster?

Will you get a fish?

Will you get a mouse?

Will you get a rabbit?

Will you get a budgie?

Will you get a guinea pig?

Will you get a stick insect?

Will you get a snake?

Will you get a lizard?

Will you get a gerbil?

Will you get a tortoise?

Will you get a parrot?

Will you get a rat?

Will you get a chick?

Is this a pet?

Look at these animals. Which animals could you see at a pet shop?

shark

rabbit

budgie

lion

Answer: Rabbits and birds can be seen at a pet shop.

What am I?

I am covered in fur.	I have four legs.
I haven't got a tail.	I am smaller than a guinea pig.

Picture glossary

chick

stick insect

Index

22

Notes for teachers and parents

Before reading

Tuning in: Talk about what pets the child has (or would like to have). What would be the best thing about having a pet?

After reading

Recall and reflection: Which pet would be the most exciting to own? Which pets would be fun to stroke?

Sentence knowledge: Help the child to count the number of words in each sentence.

Word knowledge (phonics): Encourage the child to point at the word 'get' on any page. Sound out the phonemes in the word 'g/e/t'. Ask the child to sound out each letter as they point at it and then blend the sounds together to make the word 'get'.

Word recognition: Challenge the child to race you to point at the word 'you' on any page.

Rounding off

Sing together the following song (to the tune of 'Here we go round the Mulberry Bush'):

We'll go to the pet shop to get a pet,
get a pet, get a pet.
We'll go to the pet shop to get a pet,
What pet will you get?
You could get a (choose a pet) as a pet
a xxx as a pet, a xxx as a pet.
You could get a xxx as a pet,
That's a nice pet to get.

Word coverage

Sentence stem

Will you get a _____?

High-frequency words

a
get
will
you

Ask children to read these words:

cat	p4
fish	p7
chick	p19
hamster	p6

Topic words

budgie
cat
chick
dog
fish
gerbil
guinea pig
hamster
lizard
mouse
parrot
rabbit
rat
snake
stick insect
tortoise